African Writers Series

183

The Fisherman's Invocation

The Fisherman's Invocation

GABRIEL OKARA

LONDON
HEINEMANN
NAIROBI . IBADAN . LUSAKA

Heinemann Educational Books Ltd
48 Charles Street, London W1X 8AH
PMB 5205 Ibadan   .   P.O. Box 45314 Nairobi
P.O. Box 3966 Lusaka
EDINBURGH MELBOURNE TORONTO AUCKLAND KINGSTON
SINGAPORE   HONG KONG   KUALA LUMPUR   NEW DELHI

ISBN 0 435 90183 4

Filmset in Great Britain by
Northumberland Press Ltd, Gateshead, Tyne & Wear,
and printed by
Fletcher & Son Ltd, Norwich

Contents

Introduction

A collection of Okara's poems is long overdue. Indeed, one of the ironies of the history of modern African literature, or of Nigerian literature, for that matter, is that until this moment there has been no single volume of Okara's poetry, in spite of the fact that he is one of the oldest among practising modern African poets and his poetry by general acclaim is a distinctive achievement. By a curious turn of fortune he has remained a popular anthology poet—there is hardly any anthology of African poetry that does not contain representative poems by Okara. Perhaps, the fact that he has so far existed only in anthologies is partly responsible for another deficiency in the canon of African criticism: the absence of any detailed study of his poems and his art. It could however, be argued that the non-existence of an inclusive collection of his poems precludes any full appreciation of the range and scope of his poetic arts. The purpose of *The Fisherman's Invocation* is to correct this lapse and fill a vacuum. This publication, then, can be justifiably referred to as a monumental contribution to African literature.

But its importance cannot be viewed in terms of the comprehensiveness of the volume for it is indeed a lean harvest when we think that Okara is a prolific writer who now for almost three decades has been actively writing poetry. Within this period, Okara has written thousands of poems now lost to history. We should be thinking in terms of editions of collections and selections of Okara's poetry, but alas, that must remain a wishful thought. This volume represents what has been salvaged of Okara's published poetry from anthologies, periodicals and journals, particularly *Black Orpheus* and his latest, previously unpublished poems made up of 'Franven-kirche', which was written before the Nigerian Civil War, and of nine written during and after the war. The consolation is that within these covers we have most of what the poet himself considers his best poems including the prize-winning poem 'The Call of the River Nun' that launched him on his poetic career (though he constantly laments the loss of 'The Gambler', 'I've killed the year that killed me' and 'Leave us alone to heal our wounds'—a war poem that was set to music and performed).

Okara is partly responsible for this unfortunate situation. Content for many years to create his poems, read them to audiences and live a life committed to art, he is generally careless with his manuscripts; it did not occur to him, until the civil war broke out, to put his manuscripts together. He assembled what he had of his later manuscripts and survived the war with them only to lose them in Port Harcourt in the uncertain period which immediately followed the formal cessation of hostilities. At this time there were large movements of people and life was still precarious. The loss of these manuscripts is one of the less dramatic tragedies of the Nigerian Civil War.

Born into a Christian and literate family at Bumoundi in Ekpetinma clan, Yenogoa Local Government Area of the Rivers State of Nigeria, he had his elementary school education in the local school from where he proceeded to Government College, Umuahia. The Second World War interrupted his career at Umuahia. He completed his formal secondary school education in 1940 at Yaba Higher College where he sat and passed the Senior Cambridge with an 'A' in art. A number of interesting aspects of Okara's life at this period are worth noting because they give some insight into the nature of his later writing. Okara was a voracious reader and showed keen interest in philosophy—concerned with the problems of man and human existence—music, art and literature. A fine artist, he was in particular a painter who specialised in watercolour under the tutelage of one of Nigeria's renowned artists and sculptors, Ben Enwonwu. This is a sensibility that profoundly influenced him in later years because when he eventually qualified as a professional book-binder he conceived of it more as a creative art: 'Book-binding has something to do with creativity—the artistic use of the hands to produce a work of art—that's what book-binding is.' Something of the painter's instinct can be deduced from his close attention to details of scenery in his poems—the ability to create an atmosphere, a mood or a situation is one of the characteristics of his poetic style. Everyone thought young Okara would develop fully into a famous visual or plastic artist but a strange experience which he recounts vividly after so many years changed the course of his creative genius. Someone snatched his drawing pencil away from him in a dream and Herbert Macaulay gave him three big volumes of books entitled *Down, Down, Down!* From then on his interest changed from painting to writing. He wrote profusely thereafter. The manuscript is now lost, but 'The Call of the River Nun' is the best of these early efforts.

Teenage Okara was interested in reading Westerns and what fascinated him was the down-to-earth vigorous language of the stories which brought out graphically the frontier life of early America. In this respect he believes that he was probably exhibiting a natural residual likeness for violence in all humans. Nevertheless, he found the Chinese blood-baths a bit too sanguinary. Generally, Okara was interested in novels with social situations and it is not surprising that in his early life he liked Dickens. His only novel, *The Voice*, is also very much a novel of social concern, and even a casual reading of many of his poems will reveal how deeply concerned Okara is with suffering, oppression, the futility of superficial pleasure of life and the general lack of love in human relationships.

The next few years, following the end of his academic career at Higher College at Yaba, were hectic for Okara. He had brief periods as a schoolteacher at Ladilac Institute, Yaba. He then joined the Royal Air Force but had to join the BOAC auxiliary force when he could not become a pilot. The war took him to the Gambia but he soon left there under unusual circumstances. After flirting with the business world—trading in pigs across the Nigerian border—he finally settled down to a permanent job with the Government Press, Lagos, in 1946 where he was employed as a book-binder. In 1950 he was sent, together with some colleagues, to start an arm of the Press at Enugu. It was during this phase of his life that his interest in literature began to bear practical fruit partly as a result of his increased reading of, especially, the English romantic poets and his social concern which led him to write some scathing essays condemning the violation of Nigerian women by white soldiers. But it was Wordsworth's 'Spring' that spurred him on to writing poetry, and the first poem in this collection was the best among his early attempts.

This middle period of Okara's life and career was important in his development as a literary artist. He read extensively both to cultivate his mind and develop his poetic art and concept. Apart from Keats and the English lake poets, he became deeply interested in the poetry of Gerard Manley Hopkins whose idea of *inscape* (which Okara interprets as the invisible shape of things) held great fascination for him. Dylan Thomas' 'And death shall have no dominion' provided the model for Okara's 'One Night at Victoria Beach'. He was also impressed by T. S. Eliot, and in particular 'Four Quartets'. Two other aspects of this period of Okara's life need to be noted. The first is his various literary activities. He wrote many short stories almost all of which are now lost, but one of them 'The Iconoclast' won the first prize in a British Council short story competition about 1954. He also wrote profusely for radio and one of the significant pieces to come out of this period was a play about creation based on an Ijaw creation legend.

Perhaps, one of his greatest contributions to African literature and what was to give his works their distinctiveness was his interest at this time in the literary culture of his people. He was involved in the incipient cultural awakening of the period and was one of its torch bearers, giving talks on radio about the culture of African peoples. He became interested in oral traditional literature, made vast collections of it and translated some of the legends, myths and poems into English. Okara was exceedingly fascinated by the tortoise as both hero and villain and many years after is still nursing the hope of writing a *magnum opus* entitled 'The Rise and Fall of Tortoise'. The point is that the tortoise story delineates for Okara stages in the development of the human mind from the period of jungle law to the period when man became aware of his surroundings and was trying to interpret natural phenomena.

However, the important fact for us now is the impact which these diverse experiences have had on him as a modern African poet. They certainly helped to sharpen his critical and conceptual formulation of art, subsequently realised in his practice. Okara sees all art as surrealistic, advocates the use of local imagery and emphasises the magical power of words in invoking context and local atmosphere. But the really fascinating thing about Okara is that he is a natural poet. And we don't mean this in the sense of artless naïveté but rather in the way in which his sophistication and the many influences on him, foreign and traditional African, blend and do not obtrude in his writings. It is as if they had been absorbed, digested and then transmitted into new creations quite different from their originals. What is most significant, though, is that this ability is based on a native genious inherent in his African sensibility. And these poems are generally marked by alluring lyricism and superficial simplicity of diction which are reminiscent of oral traditional songs. These are the reasons even the most esoteric of his poetry appears easily accessible while making profound statements and comments. This ability to combine these two aspects of the communicative force of poetry without attracting any of the familiar accusations of incomprehensibility is the mark of Okara's greatness as a poet.

Okara's poems reflect definite stages of the country's and his personal development, but with two constants. The constants are: first, the love poems which feature at every stage of his writing career—'To A Star' and 'Celestial Songs' were composed in 1976—and, second, the reflective and plangent qualities of his poetry which not only represent a pattern of seriousness but invariably point the way to the deeper implications of these poems. Okara's early poetry deals with the period of national and personal consciousness and the problem of the conflict of cultures: such poems as 'The Call of the River Nun', 'Piano and Drums' and 'The Snowflakes Sail Gently Down' are representative of this phase of his work. The title poem, 'The Fisherman's Invocation' which is also Okara's most ambitious work, perhaps, brings this period to a close on the national level by reflecting through indigenous imagery the real traumas and tribulations of nation building.

The Nigerian Civil War was for Okara, as for most people, a sad experience. His response to the war and to its implications for the helpless victims caught in it are recorded in his war poems, which are structurally some of his best writing. These poems not only show Okara's deep feeling for human suffering, but also his ability to take in human scenes fully, for the ambiguities and ironies revealed therein go to teach us more about human life, attitudes and society. One of the poems written during the war years which does not contain an overt war theme deserves special mention. This is 'The Revolt of the Gods' (1969 but still unfinished), a satirical work which has as its burden the pervasive moral themes of Okara's poems, but is an experiment in a new mode. It is either a pointer to the poet's new style or may be a freakish effort similar to that which created 'The Fisherman's Invocation'.

The sensitive reader is struck by the poet's muffled tone of protest throughout these poems, the compassion and innocence of the wailing voice, the sage-like comments and pronouncements of a writer, the force of whose work steals up unaware as he talks to man.

Theo Vincent
Department of English
University of Lagos

The Fisherman's Invocation

The Fisherman's Invocation

I

Cast your net to the rightside
Nothing?
     Nothing

Cast it to the leftside
Nothing?
     Nothing

Then cast it to the back of the canoe
and draw gently and carefully
while I paddle the canoe forward—
Nothing?

     It's only the Back caught
     in the meshes of Today
     and I see past moons past suns
     past nights and past gods reflected
     by the Back trying to slip
     through the Meshes like a fish.

Draw gently
draw carefully
don't let it slip
draw it up into
the canoe and let's hold
it in our palms
the Back, the gods,
even for only
one still moment
one still moment
one teaching moment

3

My hands tremble
for I fear the masquerades
of the resurrecting Back

Draw man draw
Strengthen your Chest
The Front grows from the Back
like buds from a tree stump

Do buds sprout from dead stumps?
The stump of my Back is standing dead
in a desert and its essence
is with the desert sun

Your back's stump is not dead.
Deep down in the desert
there's water bubbling up to your roots
So draw, draw the Back
caught in the net into the canoe
and stretch forth your hands
into the face of the sun
and pluck down the essence
of the stump of your Back

In the face of the sun
I see only darkness
At the back of my Back
I see only darkness
and the water in the desert
has dried in darkness

No darkness no light
no light no darkness
You are seeing chicken
giving birth to a lamb
There's water at the back
of your Back gushing from a womb

4

There's no more substance
from a womb. The water
dried up after the flood
showing skeletons and dead wood

Dig deep at the back
of the womb. There's water
there's water from a river
flowing from the bottom of the Back
of the womb. So draw up the Back caught
in the net. Draw it up and let's look it over
in our insides, in our heads

The Back is my first
little paddle I lost
in the river and whose
shape I cannot now remember

Then let your head
be the head of an elephant
let your eyes be the eyes
of a leopard and stalk the Back
stalk the Back in the forest
stalk the Back in the heavens
stalk it in the earth
stalk it in your umbilical cord.

Look behind trees look behind
moon fleeing from angry sun
look behind sun with flaming
eye lashes fixed by broom of moon
and stalk it behind burnt
teeth of Cricket burnt for laughing
at Earth in water dissolving

I cannot turn my eyes
for I am caught in grim
teeth of trap of Today

Then the Front is dying
in the womb of the river
and on your laps will lie
a still-birth Front
and you'll no more go
to the ponds to fish
you'll no more throw
your net in the river.
With your dead Back
hanging on your back
and your dead Front
lying on your laps
You'll no more be man among
men; for you have defiled the Back
and the Things of the ground
and have killed the gods of the Back
So let go the Back in the net
Let your weeping gods drop
into the river and come to the prow
and I will to the bow
and I will catch the Back
and the weeping Gods in the net
and give them power
to thrust my hand into the face of the sun
as the moon with a broom and pluck down
the Essence of your dead stump
and bring forth the Child-Front.

2

(the Invocation)

See the sun in my hands
    I see
See the Gods in the sun
    I see
See the Back in my hands
    I see
See the Front in my hands
    I see

You are seeing the sun in my hands
You are seeing Gods in my hands
You are seeing the Back in my hands
You are seeing the Front in my hands

    I see
    I see

See the moon in my hands
    I see

You are seeing the moon in my hands
You are seeing the back of the womb

    I see
    I see

You are just a shape in the womb
The living shape of your Back
The living shape of the Earth

    I am
    I am

    I am just a shape in the womb
    I am just a shape of my Back
    I am just a shape of the Earth

You are just a shape of the Earth
The Earth is the womb of wombs
The sun is sperm of sperms
and the sun is playing in your front

       The sun is playing in my front
       urging my blood to the Back
       and the Front; the sun is playing
       in my front and I hear the song
       of the Back coming rushing
       rushing coming. I am wrapped
       in steps of the dancing Back
       and I can hear, I can hear the Front
       coming gently coming painfully coming

O midwifemoon rub gently down
the back of your Back
while the sun play his play
and the Back dance its dance
and assembly of mermaids
sing their bubbling water song
beneath the river waves

O play, let the sun play
and rub rub midwifemoon
down the back of the Back.
For the Front is coming gushing
coming with sound of river
rushing over a fall subduing
barriers of height and stone

And let O let the deep drums
of deep waters boom and mingle
with deep drums of deep Gods
in their play in your inside

8

Let them mingle O mingle with the clatter
of the drums of Today
for the coming, safe coming of the Front

The Front is coming
breaking through my
ruptured inside.
The Front is coming
but it's lightning
a million-tongued lightning
flashing, exploding in my head

Rumble thunder God rumble.
Stride down to the edge
of the world and rumble
until your booming voice
encircles the earth
booming until the earth
trembles in agony of birth

The Front is coming
It is a ball of fire
searing through my being
and I tremble at the full birth-course.
The earth trembles and I am wrapped
in lightning wail-song of the Front.

Stretch forth your hands
O striding Gods and temper
O temper the fireball Front
with your mystic touch. And let
O let it rest in your teaching hands
and mould it with the mould
of the back of the womb.

3
(The Child-Front)

The child-Front has come
        What child is it?
It came with the head
        What is it?
It came without teeth
        Did it come talking?
Wait, let it take form
The sun-play is not ended
        Did it not cry?
It is not yet human

        Where are your Gods now
        Gods of the Back that have
        brought forth this monster?
        Throw it away, throw it into
        the river and let the mermaids
        carry it on their songs.
        Throw it away to the Back
        and let the Back swallow it in its abyss
        And let the Gods remember their lives are in my hands

Patience man patience
The play is not ended
and midwifemoon with it in her hands
is rising on the crest of darkness
to the eye of the sky

        I want to hear no more of midwifemoon
        I want to hear no more of the back of the womb

Patience I say patience
and the spent sun is slowly climbing

climbing down a burning ladder
to regain his powers, his force
beneath smoky roofs

So do not reject the Back
and abandon your child-Front
before the sun ends his play
the Back its moulding dance
the mermaids their water song
and midwifemoon her rise

Sleep with a sweet inside and dream
for the sun will rise singing
and midwifemoon will come down smiling
and deliver into your hands in your dream
a child a human child that will not burn your hands.

So let's fish no more.
Steer the canoe to our hearths
and let's warm ourselves
with the songs of the Back and songs
of the coming Front entwined
like tendrils in our insides
to await the coming of midwifemoon

4
(Birth Dance of the Child-Front)

Let's dance with feet
that yesterday knows
and sing with voice
that breaks into tomorrow

      Let's dance let's sing
      Let's sing and dance

for the great child-Front
has come is coming

Let's drink and dance
let palmwine flow
like the Niger flow
and raise our feet
and shake the ground

Let's dance let's sing
Let's sing and dance
for the great child-Front
has come is coming

Let your feet be
knowing-something feet
and let your voice be
knowing-something voice

Let's dance let's sing
let's sing and dance
for the great child-Front
has come is coming

Let's dance with rhythms
of things of the Front
Raise the dead with song and dance
raze to the ground all thwarting things.

Let's dance let's sing
let's sing and dance
for the great child-Front
has come is coming

Let's leaven our dance
of the Front with rhythms
of the Back and strengthen
the fragile songs of the new
with songs of mermaids

So roll your eyes
and sway your hips
to the Back and Front
Raise your voice
to the eye of the sky
with songs that are tall and strong

Let's dance let's sing
Let's sing and dance
for the great child-Front
has come is coming

Now song and wine
are up in our heads
and voice up in the sky
burning the sun and the moon

And so the rhythm has changed
but not the theme—
Dance in circles
sing in circles
stamp your feet
to the circular drums

Dance in circles
in endless dance
sing in circles
no beginning no end

No beginning no end
we dance and dance
to coming Fronts
to passing Fronts
without beginning without end

So dance dance
change your steps
change your songs
tie your steps
tie your songs
to the changing beat
till song and dance
and beat of drum
join in one to keep
from mischief the great child-Front

     Let's sing and dance
     in endless circles
     till song and dance
     and beat of drum join in one

Dance dance
your muscles tremble
your fingers tingle
with the spirit of the dance
and the spirit of the Front

     Let's dance let's sing
     let's sing and dance
     for the great child-Front
     has come is coming

5

The celebration is now ended
but the echoes are all around
whirling like a harmattan
whirl-wind throwing dust around
and hands cover faces and feet grope

The celebration is now ended
the drums lie quiet, silent, waiting.
And the dancers disperse, walking
with feet that have known many dances
waiting for the next; walking
with their hearts climbing up their feet
to their places and the palmwine descending
from their heads to settle in their bellies
and their bodies turn cold. For the spirit
of the dance has left and their faces become naked.

But the child-Front is now lying on laps
feeding from measureless breasts of the Back
Singing green lullabys which tingle our heads.
And we learn to sing half familiar half strange songs
We learn to dance to half familiar half strange
rhythms fashioned in dreams as the child-Front
Lay sleeping with breasts in his mouth.

The Call of the River Nun

I hear your call!
I hear it far away;
I hear it break the circle
of these crouching hills.

I want to view your face
again and feel your cold
embrace; or at your brim
to set myself and
inhale your breath; or
Like the trees, to watch
my mirrored self unfold
and span my days with
song from the lips of dawn.

I hear your lapping call!
I hear it coming through;
invoking the ghost of a child
listening, where river birds hail
your silver-surfaced flow.

My river's calling too!
Its ceaseless flow impels
my found'ring canoe down
its inevitable course.
And each dying year
brings near the sea-bird call,
the final call that
stills the crested waves
and breaks in two the curtain
of silence of my upturned canoe.

O incomprehensible God!
Shall my pilot be
my inborn stars to that
final call to Thee
O my river's complex course?

Once Upon a Time

Once upon a time, son,
they used to laugh with their hearts
and laugh with their eyes;
but now they only laugh with their teeth,
while their ice-block-cold eyes
search behind my shadow.

There was a time indeed
they used to shake hands with their hearts;
but that's gone, son.
Now they shake hands without hearts
while their left hands search
my empty pockets.

'Feel at home'! 'Come again';
they say, and when I come
again and feel
at home, once, twice,
there will be no thrice—
for then I find doors shut on me.

So I have learned many things, son.
I have learned to wear many faces
like dresses—homeface,
officeface, streetface, hostface,
cocktailface, with all their conforming smiles
like a fixed portrait smile.

And I have learned, too,
to laugh with only my teeth
and shake hands without my heart.
I have also learned to say, 'Goodbye',
when I mean 'Good-riddance';

to say 'Glad to meet you',
without being glad; and to say 'It's been
nice talking to you', after being bored.

But believe me, son.
I want to be what I used to be
when I was like you. I want
to unlearn all these muting things.
Most of all, I want to relearn
how to laugh, for my laugh in the mirror
shows only my teeth like a snake's bare fangs!

So show me, son,
how to laugh; show me how
I used to laugh and smile
once upon a time when I was like you.

Piano and Drums

When at break of day at a riverside
I hear jungle drums telegraphing
the mystic rhythm, urgent, raw
like bleeding flesh, speaking of
primal youth and the beginning,
I see the panther ready to pounce,
the leopard snarling about to leap
and the hunters crouch with spears poised;

And my blood ripples, turns torrent,
topples the years and at once I'm
in my mother's lap a suckling;
at once I'm walking simple
paths with no innovations,
rugged, fashioned with the naked
warmth of hurrying feet and groping hearts
in green leaves and wild flowers pulsing.

Then I hear a wailing piano
solo speaking of complex ways
in tear-furrowed concerto;
of far-away lands
and new horizons with
coaxing diminuendo, counterpoint,
crescendo. But lost in the labyrinth
of its complexities, it ends in the middle
of a phrase at a daggerpoint.

And I lost in the morning mist
of an age at a riverside keep
wandering in the mystic rhythm
of jungle drums and the concerto.

Were I To Choose

When Adam broke the stone
and red streams raged down to
gather in the womb,
an angel calmed the storm;

And, I, the breath mewed
in Cain, unblinking gaze
at the world without
from the brink of an age

That draws from the groping lips
a breast-muted cry
to thread the years.
(O were I to choose)

And now the close of one
and thirty turns, the world
of bones is Babel, and
the different tongues within
are flames the head
continually burning.

And O of this dark halo
were the tired head free.

And when the harmattan
of days has parched the throat
and skin, and sucked the fever
of the head away,

Then the massive dark
descends, and flesh and bone
are razed. And (O were I to choose) I'd cheat the worms
and silence seek in stone.

Spirit of the Wind

The storks are coming now—
white specks in the silent sky.
They had gone north seeking
fairer climes to build their homes
when here was raining.

They are back with me now—
Spirits of the wind,
beyond the god's confining
hands they go north and west and east,
instinct guiding.

But willed by the gods
I'm sitting on this rock
watching them come and go
from sunrise to sundown, with the spirit
urging within.

And urging a red pool stirs,
and each ripple is
the instinct's vital call,
a desire in a million cells
confined.

O God of the gods and me,
shall I not heed
this prayer-bell call, the moon
angelus, because my stork is caged
in Singed Hair and Dark Skin?

New Year's Eve Midnight

Now the bells are tolling—
A year is dead.
And my heart is slowly beating
the Nunc Dimittis
to all my hopes and mute
yearnings of a year
and ghosts hover round
dream beyond dream

Dream beyond dream
mingling with the dying
bell-sounds fading
into memories
like rain drops
falling into a river.

And now the bells are chiming—
A year is born.
And my heart-bell is ringing
in a dawn.
But it's shrouded things I see
dimly stride
on heart-canopied paths
to a riverside.

You Laughed
and Laughed
and Laughed

In your ears my song
is motor car misfiring
stopping with a choking cough;
and you laughed and laughed and laughed.

In your eyes my ante-
natal walk was inhuman, passing
your 'omnivorous understanding'
and you laughed and laughed and laughed.

You laughed at my song,
you laughed at my walk.

Then I danced my magic dance
to the rhythm of talking drums pleading, but you shut your
eyes and laughed and laughed and laughed.

And then I opened my mystic
inside wide like
the sky, instead you entered your
car and laughed and laughed and laughed.

You laughed at my dance,
you laughed at my inside.

You laughed and laughed and laughed.
But your laughter was ice-block
laughter and it froze your inside froze
your voice froze your ears
froze your eyes and froze your tongue.

And now it's my turn to laugh;
but my laughter is not
ice-block laughter. For I
know not cars, know not ice-blocks.

My laughter is the fire
of the eye of the sky, the fire
of the earth, the fire of the air,
the fire of the seas and the
rivers fishes animals trees
and it thawed your inside,
thawed your voice, thawed your
ears, thawed your eyes and
thawed your tongue.

So a meek wonder held
your shadow and you whispered:
'Why so?'
And I answered:
'Because my fathers and I
are owned by the living
warmth of the earth
through our naked feet.'

The Mystic Drum

The mystic drum beat in my inside
and fishes danced in the rivers
and men and women danced on land
to the rhythm of my drum

But standing behind a tree
with leaves around her waist
she only smiled with a shake of her head.

Still my drum continued to beat,
rippling the air with quickened
tempo compelling the quick
and the dead to dance and sing
with their shadows—

But standing behind a tree
with leaves around her waist
she only smiled with a shake of her head.

Then the drum beat with the rhythm
of the things of the ground
and invoked the eye of the sky
the sun and the moon and the river gods—
and the trees began to dance,
the fishes turned men
and men turned fishes
and things stopped to grow—

But standing behind a tree
with leaves around her waist
she only smiled with a shake of her head.

And then the mystic drum
in my inside stopped to beat—
and men became men,
fishes became fishes
and trees, the sun and the moon
found their places, and the dead
went to the ground and things began to grow.

And behind the tree she stood
with roots sprouting from her
feet and leaves growing on her head
and smoke issuing from her nose
and her lips parted in her smile
turned cavity belching darkness.

Then, then I packed my mystic drum
and turned away; never to beat so loud any more.

One Night
at Victoria Beach

The wind comes rushing from the sea,
the waves curling like mambas strike
the sands and recoiling hiss in rage
washing the Aladuras' feet pressing hard
on the sand and with eyes fixed hard
on what only hearts can see, they shouting
pray, the Aladuras pray; and coming
from booths behind, compelling highlife
forces ears; and car lights startle pairs
arm in arm passing washer-words back
and forth like haggling sellers and buyers—

Still they pray, the Aladuras pray
with hands pressed against their hearts
and their white robes pressed against
their bodies by the wind; and drinking
palmwine and beer, the people boast
at bars at the beach. Still they pray.

They pray, the Aladuras pray
to what only hearts can see while dead
fishermen long dead with bones rolling
nibbled clean by nibbling fishes, follow
four dead cowries shining like stars
into deep sea where fishes sit in judgement;
and living fishermen in dark huts
sit round dim lights with Babalawo
throwing their souls in four cowries
on sand, trying to see tomorrow.

Still, they pray the Aladuras* pray
to what only hearts can see behind
the curling waves and the sea, the stars
and the subduing unanimity of the sky
and their white bones beneath the sand.

And standing dead on dead sands,
I felt my knees touch living sands—
but the rushing wind killed the budding words.

* Aladuras: a Christian sect addicted to ritual bathing.

The Snowflakes
Sail Gently Down

The snowflakes sail gently
down from the misty eye of the sky
and fall lightly on the
winter-weary elms. And the branches
winter-stripped and nude, slowly
with the weight of the weightless snow
bow like grief-stricken mourners
as white funeral cloth is slowly
unrolled over deathless earth.
And dead sleep stealthily from the
heater rose and closed my eyes with
the touch of silk cotton on water falling.

Then I dreamed a dream
in my dead sleep. But I dreamed
not of earth dying and elms a vigil
keeping. I dreamed of birds, black
birds flying in my inside, nesting
and hatching on oil palms bearing suns
for fruits and with roots denting the
uprooters' spades. And I dreamed the
uprooters tired and limp, leaning on my roots—
their abandoned roots
and the oil palms gave them each a sun.

But on their palms
they balanced the blinding orbs
and frowned with schisms on their
brows—for the suns reached not
the brightness of gold!

Then I awoke. I awoke
to the silently falling snow
and bent-backed elms bowing and
swaying to the winter wind like
white-robed Moslems salaaming at evening
prayer, and the earth lying inscrutable
like the face of a god in a shrine.

Adhiambo

I hear many voices
like it's said a madman hears;
I hear trees talking
like it's said a medicine man hears.

Maybe I'm a madman
I'm a medicine man.
Maybe I'm mad,
for the voices are luring me,
urging me from the midnight
moon and the silence of my desk
to walk on wave crests across a sea.

Maybe I'm a medicine man
hearing talking saps,
seeing behind trees;
but who's lost his powers
of invocation.

But the voices and the trees
are now a name-spelling and one figure
silence-etched across
the moonface is walking, stepping
over continents and seas.

And I raised my hand—
my trembling hand, gripping
my heart as handkerchief
and waved and waved—and waved—
but she turned her eyes away.

To Paveba

When young fingers stir
the fire smouldering in my inside
the dead weight of dead years rolls
crashing to the ground
and the fire begins to flame anew,

The fire begins to flame anew
devouring the debris of years—
the dry harmattan-sucked trees,
the dry tearless faces
smiling weightless smiles like breath
that do not touch the ground.

The fire begins to flame anew
and I laugh and shout to the eye
of the sky on the back of a fish
and I stand on the wayside
smiling the smile of budding trees
at men and women whose insides
are filled with ashes, who
tell me, 'We once had our flaming fire'.

Then I remember my vow.
I remember my vow not to let
my fire flame any more. And the dead
years rise creaking from the ground
and file slowly into my inside
and shyly push aside the young fingers
and smother the devouring flame.

And as before the fire smoulders in water,
continually smouldering beneath
the ashes with things I dare not tell
erupting from the hackneyed lore
of the beginning. For they die in the telling.

So let them be. Let them smoulder.
Let them smoulder in the living fire beneath the ashes.

'*Franvenkirche*'

(Our Lady's Cathedral, Munich)

I am standing on an age which is now
an object of curiosity and wonder
and which has withstood centuries
and perfected means of destruction.

I am indeed standing on Faith
absolute Faith, twin-towered Faith
in which echoes of whispered prayers
clinging to the walls give one a feeling
strange yet not strange. A feeling
which knows no language no creed
and running through my inside
to my hands made them one
with those that set brick upon brick
to build this memorial, this symbol of Faith
and landmark to this city of Munich

Munich, 1963

Moon in the Bucket

Look!
Look out there
in the bucket
the rusty bucket
with water unclean

Look!
A luminous plate is floating—
the Moon, dancing to the gentle night wind
Look! all you who shout across the wall
with a million hates. Look at the dancing moon
It is peace unsoiled by the murk
and dirt of this bucket war.

Suddenly the Air Cracks

Suddenly the air cracks
with striking cracking rockets
guffaw of bofors stuttering LMGs
jets diving shooting glasses dropping
breaking from lips people diving
under beds nothing bullets flashing fire
striking writhing bodies and walls—

Suddenly there's silence—
And a thick black smoke
rises sadly into the sky as the jets
fly away in gruesome glee—

Then a babel of emotions, voices
mothers fathers calling children
and others joking shouting 'where's your bunker?'
laughing teasing across streets
and then they gaze in groups without sadness
at the sad smoke curling skywards—

Again suddenly, the air cracks
above rooftops cracking striking
rockets guffawing bofors stuttering LMGs
ack ack flacks diving jets
diving men women dragging children
seeking shelter not there breathless
hugging gutters walls houses
crumbling rumbling thunder
bombs hearts thumping heads low
under beds moving wordless lips—

Then suddenly there's silence—
and the town heaves a deep sigh
as the jets again fly away and the guns
one by one fall silent and the gunners
dazed gaze at the empty sky, helpless—

And then voices shouting calling
voices, admiring jet's dive
pilots' bravery blaming gunners
praising gunners laughing people
wiping sweat and dust from hair
neck and shirt with trembling hands.

Things soon simmer to normal
hum and rhythm as danger passes
and the streets are peopled
with strolling men and women
boys and girls on various errands
walking talking laughing smiling—
and children running with arms
stretched out in front playing
at diving jets zoom past
unsmiling bombing rocketing shooting
with mouths between startled feet.

This also passes as dusk descends
and a friendly crescent moon
appears where the jets were.
Then simmering silence—the day passes—
And the curling black smoke,
the sadless hearts and the mangled
bodies stacked in the morgue
become memorials of this day.

Expendable Name

I am only a name
a name in the air
intruding into your peace
like an unpleasant noise
and not of flesh and blood—
flesh and blood clinging
to your bones and running
in your veins.

I am only an episode
in the morning papers
which you put aside
or throw into waste paper baskets
and turn to your bacon and egg
and milk for your young
while I whom you have
drained of flesh and blood
tread with bare feet on thorns
in bushes searching, searching
for tiny snails and insects
for my young with swollen feet.

I am only a name
an expendable name
not of the human folds
and while collapsing children
gasp their last breath
by waysides and mothers'
saltless tears form streams
on my face; and while
I am drenched with stench
of blood and rotting flesh

I am only expendable name
thrown back and forth
in ritual jokes in corridors
of sacrificial shrines
and not for your ears
for that would break the spell
which makes me only a name
as we stagger, my young and I
with nothing between skin and bone
into the gathering darkness.

Yet my heart sings of the day,
the day bursting with song
and the smile of my young
yes, my heart sings in this darkness
of the moaning, dying
dying because the spell
makes me only a name
an expendable name.

Yet my heart sings
as I weakly genuflect
to the calling Angelus bells
which reach out to me like
hands out of the gathering darkness

Cancerous Growth

The noon sun
shrivels tender buds
today's wanton massacre
burns up tender words
and from the ashes
hate is growing, forcing its way
like mushroom through yielding soil
But it's an alien growth
a cancer that destroys its host.

Umuahia, 13 December 1968

Freedom Day

It is twenty years ago today
it's twenty years ago, they said
the gods with their godly wands
broke the chains that manacled
man to man's ideologies
and so broke man's hold on man
It's twenty years ago

But look whenever you will—
North, South, East and West of the globe
look wherever you will
the same gods like hogs are shoving
squealing each other deaf
with snouts deep in blood
seeking happiness, sustenance
from Man's plaintive stream
of cries, cries tugging at the chains
broken twenty years ago.

Umuahia, 1968

Rural Path

Tunnel of dreams, dreaming tunnel
of powdery sand, soft to footfall, moonfall
filtering through windless air and silent leaves—
this green peace of rural path through green walls of moss
silences bludgeoning fears and nagging primal instinct.
For soft sand and night sounds—this path
of light and shadow smother harshness of a whimsical day.

Yet this night of peace in light and darkness
with these sounds and fireflies, winking like stars
in the bushes; this night will run its course
and tomorrow will pronounce idiom of war and death
mingled with mating calls of mating birds at dawn
to efface this abbreviated peace in dreaming
tunnel dappled with light and shadow dripping
from leaves, silent drooping leaves in moondrenched dreams.

Ogwa, 1969

Silent Girl

Sweet silent girl
what makes you speak not
what makes you speak not
of our days, and the days before?
what makes you speak not but only in silence
with your lips tight and tongue pressed against
your teeth by your pressing thoughts?
Is it because of the sneering, nagging present?
the present that has scotched yams, corn and minds,
the present that has turned babies to adults
and adults to babies, babbling babies
learning how to crawl and walk—
the present that has turned night sounds
of rural peace to sounds of exploding shells
and rattling guns and raucous laughter of death
and days of promise to heavy heart crushing days;
The present that has dried us all of emotion
and the youth of youth like harmattan the trees of living sap.
Let's break with the past that bred the present
and let today be reminder of tomorrow
though tomorrow may only be a dream
as dream may vanish in our waking
or may survive—you, the silent one or me who sings.
So be silent sweet girl
I'll be silent, speak in silence,
and let's recline on tomorrow of our dream
in the shadows of our silent thoughts
away from the hot sneering days.

Ogwa, 1969

Cross on the Moon

It is a moonlit night
the trees droop with leaves
heavy with cooling dew
gently reflect the moon descending
on soft hedges where comes forth
the screech of gleeful crickets
and the winking fire of fireflies.
Above, the 'plane circling, waits its turn
humming down hope into hearts
as it crosses again and again the circle of moon
then suddenly it stopped, it remained still—
it turned a cross on the moon
A testimony of Man's humanity breaking its bonds
and sallying forth into dangers known and unknown
to spread succour to those in their last sleep
and whose hopes have dried in parched
throats and whimpering children
on backs of fearless mothers.

Ogwa, 1969

Rain Lullaby

Sooth me not to sleep gentle rain
with your lullaby on eager
yam and cassava leaves and on
pan roof drumming beats of love
For now is not time for sleep or love
or tender emotions of days gone by
When the earth, sun and moon
juggled night and day in my head
which now is home for vampires
and silent bats flitting from wall
to wall preying on my essence
Now is time to record wickedness
bursting far and near by day
and the hum and rhythm of bravery in mercy
high in the sky at night dropping
milk in drops into open mouths
open like baby birds waiting
for feed from mother birds.

Come,
Come and Listen

Come sit with me awhile
away from your golden crowns,
pause awhile from poking the fire
beneath the burning funeral pyre
and listen to the song beyond the flames
set by trembling hands to drown my cry.
Come, sit with me you who proudly fly
beyond the heaven on eagle's wings—
Listen to flame-song beyond the flames.

Come, O come, with me awhile
you who built my pyre with hasty hands
and listen to the song gurgling through
molten lead poured down my throat
song sung with tongues of impatient flames
threading me like beads round the neck
of struggling centuries. Come, come and listen!

Come and listen to whimpered songs
of charred stumps of promise tied to mothers' backs
trembling, rooted to the ground in pouring rain—
waiting, waiting with hands raised skywards
to mercy buzzing in serene clouds.

Come, sit with me you who proudly fly
beyond the heavens on eagle's wings—
Listen to whimpered song beyond flames.
Seeking not seeking the end
of tremulous hopes men stopper ears
to strident slogans and take refuge

in primal instinct move eyes to occiputs
to see vista back to wombs, but unreceptive,
indignant wombs. So they turn back, evading
eyes of children, unopen leaves of a tendril dying.
Come with me and listen
to the rattle of dying tendrils.

O come with me awhile
you who drew triggers with tongues
up in the clouds, traversing continents and seas
and taught self-emasculation as propitiation
of your aspiring godship of the universe,
come and drink the hot song of blood
served up on green cocoyam leaves which knew
once only globes of cooling dew
Come, come and drink with the wafer
of my hopes and savour your deeds!
I will rise wise and seek mercy from the eyes
of shrivelled innocence, asking questions I cannot
now answer.

Ogwa, 1969

The Glowering Rat

This garden city lumbering out of a bad dream
sees ghosts in cooling wind and untended roses
struggling each to consummate its being.
And these puddles, these festering wounds
in streets and in my emptiness
over which my feet and mind totter
are presences cast like a shadow over my
every step; for a glowering Rat holds at bay
the spirit seeking its wonted lodgement.

But the spirit comes again and again
like homing bird, this spirit
with its wounded wings knocking coded
rhythms on resounding door, echoing
in capering hollowness; and again and again
the glowering Rat holds it at bay with bared
fangs and restive claws whetted on yester-years.
And so dispossessed, the spirit waits restless
as unrecorded days pass into grumbling days
through fingers like drops of water into a turbulent river.

Port Harcourt, May 1970

The Dead a Spirit Demands

The dead a spirit demands
from the quick
in walls set
with mortar spewing words
from half-open lips,
A spirit that
these walls would break
and close their spittle specked
lips that despoil the land.
Yes, the dead such a spirit demands!

Christmas 1971

The name is strange, not strange
but not thoughts of love and peace
which have now donned
Simpleton's robes.
And caricatured, maligned
taunted and rejected
they ride in state on deriding tongues
with crown of thorns
forced on their heads
by gods assaulted and
by hidden fears of love and peace.
But love and peace will surely sprout skywards like a sapling
straight and strong from land
dripping with water from Pilate's hands.

Flying Over the Sahara

1
Sand, sand, only dry sand
and scraggy rocks like
leprous fingers clawing at the 'plane
for a hold to pluck it down.
Here all is dead
Even the wind is dead
or ought to be dead.
But the immortal mind
with its nimble fingers
has weaned from the bowels
of the earth oil in flames
and dark smoke curling
upwards fuels his mind
and machines to build
and destroy, to nurture life and kill.

2
Dry rocks below rocking 'plane
with skeletons of water that were
winding between gorges like groping
mind in eternal search for fulfilment.
For how long this search only the waters
know, sucked away by craving sands
and only the weary dead know
consumed by implacable time.

Sunday

Shards of broken rays
through palm fronds
from rising sun face
hidden behind purple clouds;
birds' songs piercing the morning
babel of sounds of cars and voices
Babies' and hawkers' cries
and unspoken words and smiles
stamped on lips and wishes
masking reality of the day
I wake with half dead prayers
falling limply out of my lips
to the belated watchman striking the hour.

I wake with half dead prayers
with blinking eyes gauging
the sharpness of the shards of light
through sharp edged blades of louvres
groan with lost dreams lost
in fading darkness and approaching
light with light steps silent
walking on still stream

Then church bells chime prayer hour
And the preacher with stern and solemn
mien steps on lectern to address
the faithful men and women in Sunday dress
of gold damask lace and silk
smoothing folds and creases
straightening ties and collars, freeze
the word on the preacher's lips.

Dispensing Morning Balm

Dispensing morning balm
in crystal drops of songs
into the yawning city
and the rumble and asthmatic
whizzing of a young day,
these birds erase dreams
and nightmares of the fading darkness.

To a Star

I strain my tired voice in song
to reach up to the star by the moon
a song I vowed never more to sing;
But from sundown to sunrise
I seek a union continually
which breaks my vow and I sing
a silent song to the rhythm of ageing drums
drums not heeding constraints of fear
Bear the song tenderly toward an ear

But enfeebled by layers of falling years
the muted song reaches not the star

Still with a beggar's persistence I sing
vainly seeking harmony with song and drum
drum waxing louder, fed by each passing day
But it echoes only in the hills of dead years
and reaches not the STAR by the moon

Yet I dare to hope for a confluence of songs
    Mine enfeebled, sluggish
    The STAR's bright, engulfing
This song of creation in my head revolving

2

Who can stop this sacred song
that chains heart to heart?
this song that defies the seer
    hard to hear?
This song that forbids discord
but thrives in lasting accord?

O let not this be as those
which lie scotched like rose
trampled by passing years
Before it reaches the STAR

3
I am tired, tired!
my trembly feet drag.
Those in blood-bond
pass me by in their dream
And I, chastened by their passing
Drag my tired feet along
in pursuit of my own dream.

Celestial Song

1

Your song is celestial song
and so in 'different plane'
mine is terrestial song
and so is vain
vain, but it seeks ceaselessly
like rushing water the sea.
Let yours come down in drips
in crystal drips of starry light
to illumine the approaching night.

2

My song vainly climbs
like smoke from humble hearths.
It rises from lowly depths
to reach up to your song
but it is muffled by racing clouds.
So let yours come down in drips
just in drips, drips of starry song
To strengthen my trembly feet.

The Revolt of the Gods

1

1st God   We have died again and again
and have risen again and again
only to die again and again
in the dying whims of erratic modes
of man when man began and we
began with him countless centuries ago.
Since then we have owned the world
lost it, regained it and lost it
to the reckless mind of man.
He throws us to the mud, picks us up
refurbishes us, puts us in masks
stifling us, debases us in other guises
defaces us; gives us all powers
and takes them away,
as the mood catches him;
and kills us as sacrifice to his groping mind.

2nd God   We grope along with man's mind
and go whither it bids us go and do
what it bids us do, helpless like
these clouds that clothe us, driven
hither and thither by the wind.
And now he bids us die. And we must die!

2

Old God   It's death not sudden or final
as you know. But as always it's suspension
in mists of suffocating doubts
which swing us high up to the heavens
and down to the very dust he tramples on.
And for centuries we've lived in this fashion
We've lived in the twilight of life and death.

Young God	Must you allow yourselves to die thus and live thus. Must you man's plaything remain to be discarded and retrieved at will? Man is a child. He must be controlled and guided. Power is burning in our hands like the sun Or have you by your quiescence changed roles and he is now your master?

Old God	You speak like the young of god
	or man. By the grace or curse of man
	you came into being only a thousand years ago
	Many there were like you who died
	before they came or lived only
	a while and died in ignorance
	or simply wasted away for lack of sacrifices.
	Those who man loves are ageless.
	Those who he hates die ageless.
	Before long you will see this like the black
	cloud over there. We are powerless with all our
	   power.
	We are powerless with our lightning and
	   thunder.

2nd God	Man's love is our curse His hatred is our grace!
Young God	I can strike him down at will I can set fear on him like fire I can make him do my will I can make him weep and still his restless brain and bemoan his inadequacy And tears will gut his face like streams the face of the earth. All this power is you and I. You and I

own the world, the universe and we
step from planet to planet like the
steps on stones to cross a stream.
Yet, yet all this power, you say is useless—
Now look down there and see him
to whom you raise pleading hands.

(*The old gods peer down and there on earth*
man kneeling on dust, face upturned
with hands clasped
on his chest in sorrow and anguish
is praying for the life of his dying child, dying
before a shrine.)

See now, see now on whom you
dissipate your powers in plaintive words
endowing him with powers beyond him
making him bigger than himself
See him melting in anguish
like palm oil in fire
Hear him crying, moaning
See his prayers spiralling up
like a bubble from sea's bottom.
This is man you worship in your dotage.

2nd God   Impetuousness of youth is the wisdom of age.

1st God   Storm agitates sea into restless waves
               Youth impels man or god into rashness.

Young God   We are gods of the heavens and the universe
               Man and his abode are but a grain of sand
               in a desert, a drop of water in the limitless seas
               We drive into fury without breaths
               Our whisper strikes fear and joy into him

Our whisper caresses his mind and brain
into illusions of grandeur beside himself
And yet this grandeur with which he clothes
himself is but a feather a gentle wind
blows away at our command.

2nd God The interminable cycle of life and death
lends caution to boasts of boundless power
This truth in a million cycles
you'll find entrenched
And even now as we hold this discourse
Man is soiling our virtues, obliterating,
 burnishing
according as his convulsed mind turns and
 twists
like a blind worm on heated sand.
Now tune your ears to earth and hear
their discourse rising in fumes of wine.

(*The young god cocks his ears downwards*)

1st Man Don't tell me any more, it spoils my drink.
2nd Man The matter with you is you don't want to think.
1st Man What do you want me to think about?
You want me to go raving mad and shout
in the streets with my snout like swine?
Allow me to drink in peace. My God is my wine.
3rd Man Hear! hear! Very well spoken. Here's to you!
4th Man Now listen all of you, listen!
All Yes, yes.
4th Man I am a prophet!
2nd Man Like the prophets of old?
4th Man A prophet, a prophet
Prophet of doom! Seer of Doom!
3rd Man Hear! Hear! Well spoken. Here's to you!

61

4th Man	(*with a serious mien*) Fill my glass
2nd Man	What is your prophecy, may I ask, Prophet?
4th Man	(*sipping his drink*) Those who have ears to hear let them hear
3rd Man	Hear! hear!
4th Man	The world is coming to an end and all men should their affairs attend.
1st Man	(*cynically*) How is the world going to end?
4th Man	The gods have so decreed And I enjoin you all to heed this solemn message of the gods.
1st Man	(*laughing*) They are all duds, duds. Figments of your imagination! There are no blinking gods.
2nd Man	(*solemnly*) But there is a God, the living God of Abraham and his Son, Jehovah The God of heaven and earth
3rd Man	Hear! hear! Well spoken. Here's to you! (*Drinks*)
1st Man	Man is lord of the universe He strides from earth to moon and from moon to Mars and planets diverse If there be God or gods then he is God or gods And the world will only end when he so desires
3rd Man	Hear! hear! Well spoken. Here's to you! (*Drinks*)
4th Man	All you doubting Thomases will be thrown to the unquenchable fire of hell. Soon, before you know it.
1st Man	Thomas had a scientific mind Grow up man, grow up and free yourself from the shackles of your own creations.
3rd Man	Hear! hear! Well spoken. Here's to you! (*Drinks*)
Old God	That's how we are caught in the interminable cycle.

Young God	Nonsense.
2nd God	Even as you speak, your voice has weakened a trifle you are in earthly voices fading
Old God	There's naught in your vaunted powers, there's no choice And thus we suffer pains of a million deaths.